Congratulations: You can now enjoy many happy hours bird watching and record all your bird sightings in your own special bird journal.

Inside you can log up to 50 different birds and record all the details you want including—date, time, approx. distance, photo (if possible), weather, location and lots more of your own notes and records.

In years to come you can look back and recall many wonderful bird watching trips and the exact birds you saw that day. Being pocket size you can also slip your bird journal into your binocular case - or glove compartment for easy access.

In the event of loss whilst birding please contact….

Name:...

Contact Number: ....

Email:..

Quick View Bird Log

Date	Bird Seen

Quick View Bird Log

Date	Bird Seen

Bird Log Book

SKETCH:

NOTES:

Bird Log Book

BIRD:

DATE:

DAY:

TIME:

PHOTO TAKEN: Y/ N

DETAILS

APPROX DISTANCE:

LOCATION / HABITAT

WEATHER

BIRD DESCRIPTION

BIRD'S ACTIONS

YOUR ACTIONS

NOTES:

Bird Log Book

SKETCH:

NOTES:

Bird Log Book

BIRD:

DATE:

DAY:

TIME:

PHOTO TAKEN: Y/ N

DETAILS

APPROX DISTANCE:

LOCATION / HABITAT

WEATHER

BIRD DESCRIPTION

BIRD'S ACTIONS

YOUR ACTIONS

NOTES:

Bird Log Book

SKETCH:

NOTES:

Bird Log Book

BIRD:

DATE:

DAY:

TIME:

PHOTO TAKEN: Y/ N

DETAILS

APPROX DISTANCE:

LOCATION / HABITAT

WEATHER

BIRD DESCRIPTION

BIRD'S ACTIONS

YOUR ACTIONS

NOTES:

Bird Log Book

SKETCH:

NOTES:

Bird Log Book

BIRD:

DATE:

DAY:

TIME:

PHOTO TAKEN: Y/ N

DETAILS

APPROX DISTANCE:

LOCATION / HABITAT

WEATHER

BIRD DESCRIPTION

BIRD'S ACTIONS

YOUR ACTIONS

NOTES:

Bird Log Book

SKETCH:

NOTES:

Bird Log Book

BIRD:

DATE:

DAY:

TIME:

PHOTO TAKEN: Y/ N

DETAILS

APPROX DISTANCE:

LOCATION / HABITAT

WEATHER

BIRD DESCRIPTION

BIRD'S ACTIONS

YOUR ACTIONS

NOTES:

Bird Log Book

SKETCH:

NOTES:

Bird Log Book

BIRD:

DATE:

DAY:

TIME:

PHOTO TAKEN: Y/ N

DETAILS

APPROX DISTANCE:

LOCATION / HABITAT

WEATHER

BIRD DESCRIPTION

BIRD'S ACTIONS

YOUR ACTIONS

NOTES:

Bird Log Book

SKETCH:

NOTES:

Bird Log Book

BIRD:

DATE:

DAY:

TIME:

PHOTO TAKEN: Y/ N

DETAILS

APPROX DISTANCE:

LOCATION / HABITAT

WEATHER

BIRD DESCRIPTION

BIRD'S ACTIONS

YOUR ACTIONS

NOTES:

Bird Log Book

SKETCH:

NOTES:

Bird Log Book

BIRD:

DATE:

DAY:

TIME:

PHOTO TAKEN: Y/ N

DETAILS

APPROX DISTANCE:

LOCATION / HABITAT

WEATHER

BIRD DESCRIPTION

BIRD'S ACTIONS

YOUR ACTIONS

NOTES:

Bird Log Book

SKETCH:

NOTES:

Bird Log Book

BIRD:

DATE:

DAY:

TIME:

PHOTO TAKEN: Y/ N

DETAILS

APPROX DISTANCE:

LOCATION / HABITAT

WEATHER

BIRD DESCRIPTION

BIRD'S ACTIONS

YOUR ACTIONS

NOTES:

Bird Log Book

SKETCH:

NOTES:

Bird Log Book

BIRD:

DATE:

DAY:

TIME:

PHOTO TAKEN: Y/ N

DETAILS

APPROX DISTANCE:

LOCATION / HABITAT

WEATHER

BIRD DESCRIPTION

BIRD'S ACTIONS

YOUR ACTIONS

NOTES:

Bird Log Book

SKETCH:

NOTES:

Bird Log Book

BIRD:

DATE:

DAY:

TIME:

PHOTO TAKEN: Y/ N

DETAILS

APPROX DISTANCE:

LOCATION / HABITAT

WEATHER

BIRD DESCRIPTION

BIRD'S ACTIONS

YOUR ACTIONS

NOTES:

Bird Log Book

SKETCH:

NOTES:

Bird Log Book

BIRD:

DATE:

DAY:

TIME:

PHOTO TAKEN: Y/ N

DETAILS

APPROX DISTANCE:

LOCATION / HABITAT

WEATHER

BIRD DESCRIPTION

BIRD'S ACTIONS

YOUR ACTIONS

NOTES:

Bird Log Book

SKETCH:

NOTES:

Bird Log Book

BIRD:

DATE:

DAY:

TIME:

PHOTO TAKEN: Y/ N

DETAILS

APPROX DISTANCE:

LOCATION / HABITAT

WEATHER

BIRD DESCRIPTION

BIRD'S ACTIONS

YOUR ACTIONS

NOTES:

Bird Log Book

SKETCH:

NOTES:

Bird Log Book

BIRD:

DATE:

DAY:

TIME:

PHOTO TAKEN: Y/ N

DETAILS

APPROX DISTANCE:

LOCATION / HABITAT

WEATHER

BIRD DESCRIPTION

BIRD'S ACTIONS

YOUR ACTIONS

NOTES:

Bird Log Book

SKETCH:

NOTES:

Bird Log Book

BIRD:

DATE:

DAY:

TIME:

PHOTO TAKEN: Y/ N

DETAILS

APPROX DISTANCE:

LOCATION / HABITAT

WEATHER

BIRD DESCRIPTION

BIRD'S ACTIONS

YOUR ACTIONS

NOTES:

Bird Log Book

SKETCH:

NOTES:

Bird Log Book

BIRD:

DATE:

DAY:

TIME:

PHOTO TAKEN: Y/ N

DETAILS

APPROX DISTANCE:

LOCATION / HABITAT

WEATHER

BIRD DESCRIPTION

BIRD'S ACTIONS

YOUR ACTIONS

NOTES:

Bird Log Book

SKETCH:

NOTES:

Bird Log Book

BIRD:

DATE:

DAY:

TIME:

PHOTO TAKEN: Y/ N

DETAILS

APPROX DISTANCE:

LOCATION / HABITAT

WEATHER

BIRD DESCRIPTION

BIRD'S ACTIONS

YOUR ACTIONS

NOTES:

Bird Log Book

SKETCH:

NOTES:

Bird Log Book

BIRD:

DATE:

DAY:

TIME:

PHOTO TAKEN: Y/ N

DETAILS

APPROX DISTANCE:

LOCATION / HABITAT

WEATHER

BIRD DESCRIPTION

BIRD'S ACTIONS

YOUR ACTIONS

NOTES:

Bird Log Book

SKETCH:

NOTES:

Bird Log Book

BIRD:

DATE:

DAY:

TIME:

PHOTO TAKEN: Y/ N

DETAILS

APPROX DISTANCE:

LOCATION / HABITAT

WEATHER

BIRD DESCRIPTION

BIRD'S ACTIONS

YOUR ACTIONS

NOTES:

Bird Log Book

SKETCH:

NOTES:

Bird Log Book

BIRD:

DATE:

DAY:

TIME:

PHOTO TAKEN: Y/ N

DETAILS

APPROX DISTANCE:

LOCATION / HABITAT

WEATHER

BIRD DESCRIPTION

BIRD'S ACTIONS

YOUR ACTIONS

NOTES:

Bird Log Book

SKETCH:

NOTES:

Bird Log Book

BIRD:

DATE:

DAY:

TIME:

PHOTO TAKEN: Y/ N

DETAILS

APPROX DISTANCE:

LOCATION / HABITAT

WEATHER

BIRD DESCRIPTION

BIRD'S ACTIONS

YOUR ACTIONS

NOTES:

Bird Log Book

SKETCH:

NOTES:

Bird Log Book

BIRD:

DATE:

DAY:

TIME:

PHOTO TAKEN: Y/ N

DETAILS

APPROX DISTANCE:

LOCATION / HABITAT

WEATHER

BIRD DESCRIPTION

BIRD'S ACTIONS

YOUR ACTIONS

NOTES:

Bird Log Book

SKETCH:

NOTES:

Bird Log Book

BIRD:

DATE:

DAY:

TIME:

PHOTO TAKEN: Y/ N

DETAILS

APPROX DISTANCE:

LOCATION / HABITAT

WEATHER

BIRD DESCRIPTION

BIRD'S ACTIONS

YOUR ACTIONS

NOTES:

Bird Log Book

SKETCH:

NOTES:

Bird Log Book

BIRD:

DATE:

DAY:

TIME:

PHOTO TAKEN: Y/ N

DETAILS

APPROX DISTANCE:

LOCATION / HABITAT

WEATHER

BIRD DESCRIPTION

BIRD'S ACTIONS

YOUR ACTIONS

NOTES:

Bird Log Book

SKETCH:

NOTES:

Bird Log Book

BIRD:

DATE:

DAY:

TIME:

PHOTO TAKEN: Y/ N

DETAILS

APPROX DISTANCE:

LOCATION / HABITAT

WEATHER

BIRD DESCRIPTION

BIRD'S ACTIONS

YOUR ACTIONS

NOTES:

Bird Log Book

SKETCH:

NOTES:

Bird Log Book

BIRD:

PHOTO TAKEN: Y/ N

DATE:

DETAILS

DAY:

APPROX DISTANCE:

TIME:

LOCATION / HABITAT

WEATHER

BIRD DESCRIPTION

BIRD'S ACTIONS

YOUR ACTIONS

NOTES:

Bird Log Book

SKETCH:

NOTES:

Bird Log Book

BIRD:

DATE:

DAY:

TIME:

PHOTO TAKEN: Y/ N

DETAILS

APPROX DISTANCE:

LOCATION / HABITAT

WEATHER

BIRD DESCRIPTION

BIRD'S ACTIONS

YOUR ACTIONS

NOTES:

Bird Log Book

SKETCH:

NOTES:

Bird Log Book

BIRD:

DATE:

DAY:

TIME:

PHOTO TAKEN: Y/ N

DETAILS

APPROX DISTANCE:

LOCATION / HABITAT

WEATHER

BIRD DESCRIPTION

BIRD'S ACTIONS

YOUR ACTIONS

NOTES:

Bird Log Book

SKETCH:

NOTES:

Bird Log Book

BIRD:

DATE:

DAY:

TIME:

PHOTO TAKEN: Y/ N

DETAILS

APPROX DISTANCE:

LOCATION / HABITAT

WEATHER

BIRD DESCRIPTION

BIRD'S ACTIONS

YOUR ACTIONS

NOTES:

Bird Log Book

SKETCH:

NOTES:

Bird Log Book

BIRD:

DATE:

DAY:

TIME:

PHOTO TAKEN: Y/ N

DETAILS

APPROX DISTANCE:

LOCATION / HABITAT

WEATHER

BIRD DESCRIPTION

BIRD'S ACTIONS

YOUR ACTIONS

NOTES:

Bird Log Book

SKETCH:

NOTES:

Bird Log Book

BIRD:

DATE:

DAY:

TIME:

PHOTO TAKEN: Y/ N

DETAILS

APPROX DISTANCE:

LOCATION / HABITAT

WEATHER

BIRD DESCRIPTION

BIRD'S ACTIONS

YOUR ACTIONS

NOTES:

Bird Log Book

SKETCH:

NOTES:

Bird Log Book

BIRD:

DATE:

DAY:

TIME:

PHOTO TAKEN: Y/ N

DETAILS

APPROX DISTANCE:

LOCATION / HABITAT

WEATHER

BIRD DESCRIPTION

BIRD'S ACTIONS

YOUR ACTIONS

NOTES:

Bird Log Book

SKETCH:

NOTES:

Bird Log Book

BIRD:

DATE:

DAY:

TIME:

PHOTO TAKEN: Y/ N

DETAILS

APPROX DISTANCE:

LOCATION / HABITAT

WEATHER

BIRD DESCRIPTION

BIRD'S ACTIONS

YOUR ACTIONS

NOTES:

Bird Log Book

SKETCH:

NOTES:

Bird Log Book

BIRD:

DATE:

DAY:

TIME:

PHOTO TAKEN: Y/ N

DETAILS

APPROX DISTANCE:

LOCATION / HABITAT

WEATHER

BIRD DESCRIPTION

BIRD'S ACTIONS

YOUR ACTIONS

NOTES:

Bird Log Book

SKETCH:

NOTES:

Bird Log Book

BIRD:

PHOTO TAKEN: Y/ N

DATE:

DETAILS

DAY:

APPROX DISTANCE:

TIME:

LOCATION / HABITAT

WEATHER

BIRD DESCRIPTION

BIRD'S ACTIONS

YOUR ACTIONS

NOTES:

Bird Log Book

SKETCH:

NOTES:

Bird Log Book

BIRD:

DATE:

DAY:

TIME:

PHOTO TAKEN: Y/ N

DETAILS

APPROX DISTANCE:

LOCATION / HABITAT

WEATHER

BIRD DESCRIPTION

BIRD'S ACTIONS

YOUR ACTIONS

NOTES:

Bird Log Book

SKETCH:

NOTES:

Bird Log Book

BIRD:

DATE:

DAY:

TIME:

PHOTO TAKEN: Y/ N

DETAILS

APPROX DISTANCE:

LOCATION / HABITAT

WEATHER

BIRD DESCRIPTION

BIRD'S ACTIONS

YOUR ACTIONS

NOTES:

Bird Log Book

SKETCH:

NOTES:

Bird Log Book

BIRD:

DATE:

DAY:

TIME:

PHOTO TAKEN: Y/ N

DETAILS

APPROX DISTANCE:

LOCATION / HABITAT

WEATHER

BIRD DESCRIPTION

BIRD'S ACTIONS

YOUR ACTIONS

NOTES:

Bird Log Book

SKETCH:

NOTES:

Bird Log Book

BIRD:

DATE:

DAY:

TIME:

PHOTO TAKEN: Y/ N

DETAILS

APPROX DISTANCE:

LOCATION / HABITAT

WEATHER

BIRD DESCRIPTION

BIRD'S ACTIONS

YOUR ACTIONS

NOTES:

Bird Log Book

SKETCH:

NOTES:

Bird Log Book

BIRD:

DATE:

DAY:

TIME:

PHOTO TAKEN: Y/ N

DETAILS

APPROX DISTANCE:

LOCATION / HABITAT

WEATHER

BIRD DESCRIPTION

BIRD'S ACTIONS

YOUR ACTIONS

NOTES:

Bird Log Book

SKETCH:

NOTES:

Bird Log Book

BIRD:

DATE:

DAY:

TIME:

PHOTO TAKEN: Y/ N

DETAILS

APPROX DISTANCE:

LOCATION / HABITAT

WEATHER

BIRD DESCRIPTION

BIRD'S ACTIONS

YOUR ACTIONS

NOTES:

Bird Log Book

SKETCH:

NOTES:

Bird Log Book

BIRD:

DATE:

DAY:

TIME:

PHOTO TAKEN: Y/ N

DETAILS

APPROX DISTANCE:

LOCATION / HABITAT

WEATHER

BIRD DESCRIPTION

BIRD'S ACTIONS

YOUR ACTIONS

NOTES:

Bird Log Book

SKETCH:

NOTES:

Bird Log Book

BIRD:

DATE:

DAY:

TIME:

PHOTO TAKEN: Y/ N

DETAILS

APPROX DISTANCE:

LOCATION / HABITAT

WEATHER

BIRD DESCRIPTION

BIRD'S ACTIONS

YOUR ACTIONS

NOTES:

Bird Log Book

SKETCH:

NOTES:

Bird Log Book

BIRD:

DATE:

DAY:

TIME:

PHOTO TAKEN: Y/ N

DETAILS

APPROX DISTANCE:

LOCATION / HABITAT

WEATHER

BIRD DESCRIPTION

BIRD'S ACTIONS

YOUR ACTIONS

NOTES:

Bird Log Book

SKETCH:

NOTES:

Bird Log Book

BIRD:

DATE:

DAY:

TIME:

PHOTO TAKEN: Y/ N

DETAILS

APPROX DISTANCE:

LOCATION / HABITAT

WEATHER

BIRD DESCRIPTION

BIRD'S ACTIONS

YOUR ACTIONS

NOTES:

Bird Log Book

SKETCH:

NOTES:

Bird Log Book

BIRD:

DATE:

DAY:

TIME:

PHOTO TAKEN: Y/ N

DETAILS

APPROX DISTANCE:

LOCATION / HABITAT

WEATHER

BIRD DESCRIPTION

BIRD'S ACTIONS

YOUR ACTIONS

NOTES:

Bird Log Book

SKETCH:

NOTES:

Bird Log Book

BIRD:

DATE:

DAY:

TIME:

PHOTO TAKEN: Y/ N

DETAILS

APPROX DISTANCE:

LOCATION / HABITAT

WEATHER

BIRD DESCRIPTION

BIRD'S ACTIONS

YOUR ACTIONS

NOTES:

Bird Log Book

SKETCH:

NOTES:

Bird Log Book

BIRD:

DATE:

DAY:

TIME:

PHOTO TAKEN: Y/ N

DETAILS

APPROX DISTANCE:

LOCATION / HABITAT

WEATHER

BIRD DESCRIPTION

BIRD'S ACTIONS

YOUR ACTIONS

NOTES:

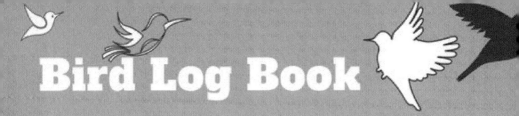

Bird Log Book

SKETCH:

NOTES:

Bird Log Book

BIRD:

DATE:

DAY:

TIME:

PHOTO TAKEN: Y/ N

DETAILS

APPROX DISTANCE:

LOCATION / HABITAT

WEATHER

BIRD DESCRIPTION

BIRD'S ACTIONS

YOUR ACTIONS

NOTES:

Bird Log Book

SKETCH:

NOTES:

Bird Log Book

BIRD:

DATE:

DAY:

TIME:

PHOTO TAKEN: Y/ N

DETAILS

APPROX DISTANCE:

LOCATION / HABITAT

WEATHER

BIRD DESCRIPTION

BIRD'S ACTIONS

YOUR ACTIONS

NOTES:

Bird Log Book

SKETCH:

NOTES:

Bird Log Book

BIRD:

DATE:

DAY:

TIME:

PHOTO TAKEN: Y/ N

DETAILS

APPROX DISTANCE:

LOCATION / HABITAT

WEATHER

BIRD DESCRIPTION

BIRD'S ACTIONS

YOUR ACTIONS

NOTES:

Bird Log Book

SKETCH:

NOTES:

Bird Log Book

BIRD:

DATE:

DAY:

TIME:

PHOTO TAKEN: Y/ N

DETAILS

APPROX DISTANCE:

LOCATION / HABITAT

WEATHER

BIRD DESCRIPTION

BIRD'S ACTIONS

YOUR ACTIONS

NOTES:

Bird Log Book

SKETCH:

NOTES:

Bird Log Book

BIRD:

DATE:

DAY:

TIME:

PHOTO TAKEN: Y/ N

DETAILS

APPROX DISTANCE:

LOCATION / HABITAT

WEATHER

BIRD DESCRIPTION

BIRD'S ACTIONS

YOUR ACTIONS

NOTES:

Bird Log Book

SKETCH:

NOTES:

Bird Log Book

BIRD:

DATE:

DAY:

TIME:

PHOTO TAKEN: Y/ N

DETAILS

APPROX DISTANCE:

LOCATION / HABITAT

WEATHER

BIRD DESCRIPTION

BIRD'S ACTIONS

YOUR ACTIONS

NOTES:

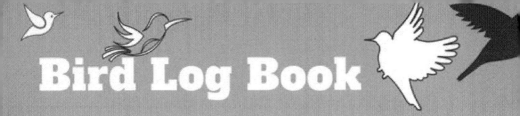

Bird Log Book

SKETCH:

NOTES:

Bird Log Book

BIRD:

DATE:

DAY:

TIME:

PHOTO TAKEN: Y/ N

DETAILS

APPROX DISTANCE:

LOCATION / HABITAT

WEATHER

BIRD DESCRIPTION

BIRD'S ACTIONS

YOUR ACTIONS

NOTES:

Thank you—Please Help...

 Thank you so much for purchasing this journal. I truly hope you find it useful and you have every success using it.

I would be delighted if you could please spare 2 minutes and leave a brief review of this journal on Amazon. It helps me enormously.

Simply visit Amazon and type in the name of this book.

"Bird journal notebook— Bird watcher's log and diary"

Find the book and click the link. Then scroll down to where you will see the reviews (there might not be any if it's a new book). Click the 'Write Customer Review' button and leave your review.

Write a customer review

That's it—it will take about 2 minutes and I will massively appreciate it. It will help such a lot. Thank you again,

Best wishes
Alan

Printed in Great Britain
by Amazon

36260297R10066